Tanks of WW II.

by

John Patton

Bibliografische Information der Deutschen Nationalbibliothek:
Die Deutsche Nationalbibliothek verzeichnet diese Publikation in der Deutschen
Nationalbibliografie; detaillierte bibliografische Daten sind im Internet über http://dnb.dnb.de
abrufbar.

Lektorat: John Patton
Korrektorat: John Patton
weitere Mitwirkende: John Patton

Herstellung und Verlag: BoD – Books on Demand, Norderstedt, ISBN: **9783751958233**

Content

Chapter	Side
American Tanks	11
German Tanks	25
Russian Tanks	39
British Tanks	55
Italian Tanks	76
Japanese Tanks	84

"If you want peace, prepare for war"

By purchasing this book, you support the search for missing soldiers.

Introduction

Vehicles were already used as a weapon of war in the early days. But of course one has to distinguish between the chariot of ancient times which were used by fighting warriors and actual armoured vehicles.

In the ancient world, chariots were used for both attack and defence, and their first mass deployment took place in 1285 BC, in the battle of Kadesh, on the Orontes River in what is today Syria. The Hittites confronted the Egyptians under Ramses II with 3,500 chariots. The chariots in those times had large wheels, box-shaped, high structures, a crew of three to four men, and they were usually pulled by more than two horses.

The Iliad as well as vase paintings from Greece and Ionia demonstrate that light chariots were used which were drawn by two horses and staffed by two men, a charioteer and a warrior. We are familiar with two- and four-wheel scythed chariots from this period; these had long and sharp blades on their wheel rims, which were designed to cause injuries to the enemy soldiers.

In addition to the scythed chariots, assault or siege wagons can be seen as the most likely forerunners of today's armoured tanks. The earliest example of these vehicles dates back to the ninth century BC and can be found in the British Museum in London.

New combat techniques made new solutions necessary to move these war vehicles: A greater flexibility than men pushing or horses pulling was required on the battlefield.

In 1855, J. Cowan introduced an armoured, steam-powered vehicle in the shape of a turtle, which he had designed using a tractor of the period. Cowan's idea was improved, and in 1890 an American named GH Edwards presented a steam-powered half-track vehicle featuring both wheels and chains at the same time.

The invention of the petrol motor played a crucial role in the development of armoured vehicles, which were initially designed with wheels for locomotion. The first prototypes appeared around the turn of the nineteenth to the twentieth century. Today, we would classify them as armoured reconnaissance vehicles. They were normal wheeled vehicles equipped with firearms and protective metal plates. With these vehicles from the early years of the 20th century, the experimental stage with armoured vehicles practically ends.

In the early years of the First World War, these armoured wheeled vehicles were already deployed in considerable numbers, but soon their limitations became evident when infantrymen started to protected themselves against them with trenches and barbed wire. The result was a demand for vehicles that were capable of overcoming such obstacles.

As time went by, armoured vehicles had to be continuously improved and optimised because warring nations were always finding new means to defend themselves against them. Mines, bazookas and anti-tank barriers are just a few examples of the new developments that have dominated in the battlefield until today.

Tank M 2 A1

Armament: 1 X 37 mm cannon, 6 X 7, 62 mm mg
Construction year: 1940
Manufacturer: Rock – Island – Arsenal
Length: 17, 68 ft
Wide: 8, 59 ft
Height: 9, 38 ft
Weight: 16, 92 t
Speed: 29, 82 mph
Range: 124, 27 mi
Armour: 1, 25 in
Crew: 6

Tank M 3 Grant

Armament: 1 X 75 mm cannon, 1 X 37 mm cannon
Construction year: 1940
Manufacturer: American Car & Foundry Company
Length: 19, 35 ft
Wide: 9, 02 ft
Height: 9, 90 ft
Weight: 27, 55 t
Speed: 24, 84 mph
Range: 109, 98 mi
Armour: 3 in

Tank M 3 Stuart

Armour: 1, 69 inArmament: 1 X 37 mm cannon, 3 X 7, 62 mm mg
Construction year: 1942
Manufacturer: American Car & Foundry Company
Length: 14, 63 ft
Wide: 7, 54 ft
Height: 8, 10 ft
Weight: 12, 10 t
Speed: 35, 41 mph
Range: 69, 59 mi
Crew: 4

Tank M 4 A 3 E 8 Sherman

Armament: 1 X 76 mm cannon, 1 X 12, 7 mm mg, 2 X 7, 62 mm mg
Construction year: 1944
Manufacturer: Ford Motor Company
Length: 24, 24 ft
Wide: 10, 03 ft
Height: 9, 74 ft
Weight: 31, 98 t
Speed: 29, 82 mph
Range: 111, 84 mi
Armour: 3, 14 in
Crew: 5

Tank M4 Sherman

Armament: 1 X 75 mm cannon, 1 X 12, 7 mm MG, 2 X 7, 62 mm mg
Construction year: 1942
Manufacturer: Grand – Blank – Arsenal
Length: 19, 52 ft
Wide: 8, 56 ft
Height: 8, 98 ft
Weight: 29, 52 t
Speed: 23, 61 mph
Range: 99, 41 mi
Armour: 2, 95 in
Crew: 5

Tank M 24 Chaffee

Armament: 1 X 75 mm cannon, 1 X 12, 7 mm mg, 2 X 7, 62 mm mg
Construction year: 1944
Manufacturer: GMC / Cadillac
Length: 18, 01 ft
Wide: 9, 31 ft
Height: 7, 25 ft
Weight: 17, 61 t
Speed: 34, 79 mph
Range: 96, 31 mi
Armour: 1, 41 in
Crew: 5

Tank M 26 Pershing

Armament: 1 X 90mm cannon, 2 X 7, 62 mm mg
Construction year: 1944
Manufacturer: MG / Fleer Tank Division
Length: 28, 83 ft
Wide: 11, 48 ft
Height: 9, 08 ft
Weight: 41, 04 t
Speed: 19, 88 mph
Range: 91, 96 mi
Armour: 4, 01 in
Crew: 5

Tank M 7 Priest

Armament: 1 X 105 mm cannon, 1 X 12, 7 mm mg
Construction year: 1942
Manufacturer: American Locomotive Company
Length: 19, 75 ft
Wide: 9, 44 ft
Height: 8, 33 ft
Weight: 22, 59 t
Speed: 25, 97 mph
Range: 124, 27 mi
Armour: 2, 44 in
Crew: 7

Tank M 8 Scott

Armament: 1 X 75 mm cannon, 1 X 12, 7 mm mg
Construction year: 1942
Manufacturer: Cadillac
Length: 16, 33 ft
Wide: 7, 61 ft
Height: 8, 92 ft
Weight: 16, 07 t
Speed: 36 mph
Range: 99 mi
Armour: 1, 75 in
Crew: 4

Tank M 36 Jackson

Armament: 1 X 90 mm cannon, 1 X 12, 7 mm mg
Construction year: 1944
Manufacturer: GM
Length: 19, 58 ft
Wide: 10 ft
Height: 10, 76 ft
Weight: 28, 14 t
Speed: 26, 09 mph
Range: 93, 20 mi
Armour: 4, 25 in
Crew: 5

Tank M10 Wolverine

Armament: 1 X 76, 2 mm cannon, 1 X 12, 7 mm mg
Construction year: 1942
Manufacturer: U.S. Army Ordnance Department
Length: 22, 40 ft
Wide: 10 ft
Height: 8, 43 ft
Weight: 29, 13 t
Speed: 31, 68 mph
Range: 186, 41 mi
Armour: 2, 24 in
Crew: 5

M39 Armored Utility Vehicle

Armament: 1 X 12, 7 mm mg
Construction year: 1944
Manufacturer: Cadillac
Length: 17, 32 ft
Wide: 9, 41 ft
Height: 6, 66 ft
Weight: 16, 04 t
Speed: 49, 70 mph
Range: 149,12 mi
Armour: 0, 51 in
Crew: 2 + 8

M 40 GMC

Armament: 1 X 155 mm cannon
Construction year: 1945
Manufacturer: Grand – Blank – Arsenal
Length: 29, 85 ft
Wide: 10, 33 ft
Height: 8, 85 ft
Weight: 35, 72 t
Speed: 23, 61 mph
Range: 105, 63 mi
Armour: 0, 47 in
Crew: 8

Tank M 3 Lee

Armament: 1 X 75 mm cannon, 1 X 37 mm cannon, 4 X 7, 62 mm mg
Construction year: 1941
Manufacturer: Rock – Island – Arsenal
Length: 18, 50 ft
Wide: 9, 15 ft
Height: 10, 23 ft
Weight: 26, 57 t
Speed: 26 mph
Range: 119, 92 mi
Armour: 2, 24 in
Crew: 6

Tank PKW 1 B

Armament: 2 X 7, 92 mm mg
Construction year: 1935
Manufacturer: Krupp – Henschel – Wegmann
Length: 14, 50 ft
Wide: 6, 75 ft
Height: 5, 64 ft
Weight: 5, 31 t
Speed: 24, 85 mph
Range: 86, 99 mi
Armour: 0, 51 in
Crew: 2

Tank PKW IV G

Armament: 1 X 75 mm cannon, 2 X 7, 92 mm mg
Construction year: 1943
Manufacturer: Krupp/Nibelungenwerke/Vomag
Length: 21, 75 ft
Wide: 7, 48 ft
Height: 8, 79 ft
Weight: 24, 6 t
Speed: 23, 61 mph
Range: 111, 84 mi
Armour: 1, 96 in
Crew: 5

Tank PKW V Panther D

Armament: 1 X 75 mm cannon, 1 X 7, 92 mm mg
Construction year: 1942
Manufacturer: Daimler – Benz
Length: 28, 41 ft
Wide: 10, 72 ft
Height: 9, 35 ft
Weight: 45, 76 t
Speed: 28, 58 mph
Range: 124, 27 mi
Armour: 4, 72 in
Crew: 5

Tank PKW III G

Armament: 1X 37 mm cannon, 2 X 7, 92 mm mg
Construction year: 1940
Manufacturer: Daimler – Benz
Length: 17, 65 ft
Wide: 9, 54 ft
Height: 7, 97 ft
Weight: 19, 19 t
Speed: 24, 85 mph
Range: 102, 52 mi
Armour: 1, 18 in
Crew: 5

Tank PKW VI Tiger E

Armament: 1 X 88 mm cannon, 2 X 7, 92 mm mg
Construction year: 1942
Manufacturer: Henschel
Length: 27, 72 ft
Wide: 12, 13 ft
Height: 9, 84 ft
Weight: 56, 09 t
Speed: 24, 85 mph
Range: 121, 16 mi
Armour: 3, 93 in
Crew: 5

Tank PKW VI Tiger B

Armament: 1 X 88 mm cannon, 2 X 7, 92 mm mg
Construction year: 1944
Manufacturer: Henschel
Length: 33, 72 ft
Wide: 12, 30 ft
Height: 10, 13 ft
Weight: 68, 69 t
Speed: 23, 61 mph
Range: 105, 63 mi
Armour: 5, 90 in
Crew: 5

Tank anti aircraft gun IV Wirbelwind

Armament: 4 X 20 mm mg
Construction year: 1944
Manufacturer: Henschel
Length: 17, 35 ft
Wide: 9, 67 ft
Height: 8, 92 ft
Weight: 21, 65 t
Speed: 23, 61 mph
Range: 121, 16 mi
Armour: 0, 62 in
Crew: 5

Tank anti aircraft gun IV Ostwind

Armament: 1 X 37 mm mg
Construction year: 1944
Manufacturer: Deutsche Eisenwerke
Length: 17, 35 ft
Wide: 12, 13 ft
Height: 8, 92 ft
Weight: 21, 56 t
Speed: 23, 61 mph
Range: 121, 61 mi
Armour: 0, 62 in
Crew: 5

Tank SD KFZ 250

Armament: 1 X 7, 92 mm mg
Construction year: 1940
Manufacturer: Bussing NAG
Length: 14, 96 ft
Wide: 6, 36 ft
Height: 5, 44 ft
Weight: 4, 52 t
Speed: 40, 38 mph
Range: 217,47 mi
Armour: 0, 47 in
Crew: 6

Tank SD KFZ 251

Armament: 2 X 7, 92 mm mg
Construction year: 1940
Manufacturer: Hanomag
Length: 19, 02 ft
Wide: 6, 88 ft
Height: 5, 74 ft
Weight: 7, 28 t
Speed: 32, 62 mph
Range: 198,83 mi
Armour: 0, 47 in
Crew: 2 + 10

Tank Sturmgeschütz III SD KFZ 142 /A

Armament: 1 X 75 mm cannon
Construction year: 1940
Manufacturer: Daimler – Benz
Length: 17, 65 ft
Wide: 9, 58 ft
Height: 6, 39 ft
Weight: 19, 29 t
Speed: 24, 85 mph
Range: 99, 41 mi
Armour: 1, 96 in
Crew: 4

Tank Sturmgeschütz III SD KFZ 142 /G

Armament: 1 X 75 mm cannon, 1 X 7, 92 mm mg
Construction year: 1943
Manufacturer: Daimler – Benz
Length: 22, 21 ft
Wide: 9, 67 ft
Height: 7, 08 ft
Weight: 23, 52 t
Speed: 24, 85 mph
Range: 96, 31 mi
Armour: 3, 14 in
Crew: 4

Tank Sturmhaubitze 42

Armament: 1 X 105 mm cannon, 1 X 7, 92 mm mg
Construction year: 1942
Manufacturer: Daimler – Benz AG
Length: 20, 14 ft
Wide: 9, 71 ft
Height: 7, 05 ft
Weight: 23, 53 t
Speed: 24, 85 mph
Range: 96, 31 mi
Armour: 3, 14 in
Crew: 4

Tank Sturmpanzer IV Brummbär

Armament: 1 X 150 mm cannon, 1 X 7, 92 mm mg
Construction year: 1942
Manufacturer: Altmärkische Kettenwerke
Length: 19, 45 ft
Wide: 9, 44 ft
Height: 8, 26 ft
Weight: 27, 75 t
Speed: 24, 85 mph
Range: 130, 48 mi
Armour: 3, 93 in
Crew: 5

Tank T 35

Armament: 1 X 76, 2 mm cannon, 2 X 45 mm mg, 5 X 7, 62 mm mg
Construction year: 1935
Manufacturer: Kirov – Zadov
Length: 31, 52 ft
Wide: 10, 49 ft
Height: 11, 25 ft
Weight: 40, 8 t
Speed: 18, 02 mph
Range: 93, 20 mi
Armour: 1, 18 in
Crew: 10

Tank BT 7

Armament: 1 X 45 mm cannon, 2 X 7, 62 mm mg
Construction year: 1938
Manufacturer: Komitern
Length: 18, 30 ft
Wide: 7, 97 ft
Height: 7, 18 ft
Weight: 12, 30 t
Speed: 45, 36 mph
Range: 309, 44 mil
Armour: 0, 86 in
Crew: 3

Tank T 26 S

Armament: 1 X 45 mm cannon, 2 X 7, 62 mm mg
Construction year: 1938
Manufacturer: Komitern
Length: 15, 26 ft
Wide: 8 ft
Height: 7, 64 ft
Weight: 9, 19 t
Speed: 16, 77 mph
Range: 214, 99 mi
Armour: 0, 98 in
Crew: 3

Tank KV 1C

Armament: 1 X 76, 2 mm cannon, 3 X 7, 62 mm mg
Construction year: 1941
Manufacturer: Cheljabinsk
Length: 22, 3 ft
Wide: 10, 92 ft
Height: 10, 66 ft
Weight: 41, 92 t
Speed: 18, 64 mph
Range: 108, 73 mi
Armour: 4, 72 in
Crew: 5

Tank T 40

Armament: 1 X 20 mm or 1 X 12, 7 mm mg, 7, 62 mm mg
Construction year: 1940
Manufacturer: Gorki
Length: 13, 51 ft
Wide: 7, 64 ft
Height: 6, 49 ft
Weight: 4, 91 t
Speed: 27, 96 mph
Range: 217, 47 mi
Armour: 0, 55 in
Crew: 2

Tank T 34

Armament: 1 X 85 mm cannon, 2 X 7, 62 mm mg
Construction year: 1944
Manufacturer: Chelyabinsk
Length: 26, 73 ft
Wide: 9, 74 ft
Height: 8, 92 ft
Weight: 31, 19 t
Speed: 31, 06 mph
Range: 186, 41 mi
Armour: 2, 95 in
Crew: 5

Tank JS 1

Armament: 1 X 122 mm cannon, 3 X 7, 62 mm mg
Construction year: 1943
Manufacturer: Tankograd
Length: 31, 52 ft
Wide: 10, 26 ft
Height: 8, 89 ft
Weight: 39, 66 t
Speed: 22, 99 mph
Range: 149, 12 mi
Armour: 4, 72 in
Crew: 4

Tank JS 3

Armament: 1 X 122 mm cannon, 2 X 7, 62 mm mg
Construction year: 1945
Manufacturer: Tankograd
Length: 32, 77 ft
Wide: 10, 49 ft
Height: 8, 89 ft
Weight: 40, 84 t
Speed: 22, 99 mph
Range: 130, 48 mi
Armour: 9, 05 in
Crew: 4

Tank BA 64

Armament: 1 X 7, 26 mm mg
Construction year: 1942
Manufacturer: GAZ
Length: 12 ft
Wide: 5, 65 ft
Height: 6, 28 ft
Weight: 2, 36 t
Speed: 49, 7 mph
Range: 372,82 mi
Armour: 0, 04 in
Crew: 2

Tank ZSU 37

Armament: 1 X 37 mm mg
Construction year: 1944
Manufacturer: GAZ
Length: 17, 30 ft
Wide: 9 ft
Height: 7, 2 ft
Weight: 11 t
Speed: 28 mph
Range: 220 mi
Armour: 1, 37 in
Crew: 6

Battel of Kursk 1943.

Iwojima 1945.

Sherman tanks refueling while waiting to go on
transporters,Normandy 1944.

Japanese Type 95 Ha Go tank 1944 on Peleliu 1944.

Battel of Bulge

Tank ISU 152

Armament: 1 X 152 mm cannon, 1 X 12, 7 mm mg
Construction year: 1943
Manufacturer: Tscheljabinsk
Length: 30, 10 ft
Wide: 10, 10 ft
Height: 8, 20 ft
Weight: 44, 78 t
Speed: 22, 99 mph
Range: 136, 7 mi
Armour: 4, 72 in
Crew: 5

Tank ISU 122

Armament: 1 X 120 mm cannon, 1 X 12, 7 mm mg
Construction year: 1943
Manufacturer: Tscheljabinsk
Length: 32, 4 ft
Wide: 10, 1 ft
Height: 8, 2 ft
Weight: 45, 27 t
Speed: 23 mph
Range: 140 mi
Armour: 4, 72 in
Crew: 5

Tank Katjuscha zis 6

Armament: 8 X 82 mm rocket
Construction year: 1933
Manufacturer: Moscow Zavod imeni Stalina factory
Length: 11, 03 ft
Wide: 3, 54 ft
Height: 7, 08 ft
Weight: 4, 16 t
Speed: 34, 17 mph
Range: unknown
Armour: no in
Crew: 2

Tank Mark II

Armament: 1 X 7, 92 mm mg
Construction year: 1932
Manufacturer: Vickers
Length: 12, 99 ft
Wide: 6, 00 ft
Height: 5, 51 ft
Weight: 3, 54 t
Speed: 34, 79 mph
Range: 130, 48 mi
Armour: 0, 51 in
Crew: 2

Amphibious vehicle Terrapin Mk I

Armament: no
Construction year: 1944
Manufacturer: Morris Commercial
Length: 22, 96 ft
Wide: 8, 75 ft
Height: 9, 74 ft
Weight: 6, 88 t
Speed: 14, 91 mph
Range: 149, 12 mi
Armour: 0, 31 in
Crew: 2

Tank Mark VI

Armament: 1 X 15 mm mg, 1 X 7, 92 mm mg
Construction year: 1929
Manufacturer: Vickers
Length: 12, 92 ft
Wide: 6, 75 ft
Height: 6, 98 ft
Weight: 5, 16 t
Speed: 35 mph
Range: 130 mi
Armour: 0, 55 in
Crew: 3

Tank Cruiser Mark V Covenanter

Armament: 1 X 40 mm cannon, 1 X 7, 92 mm mg
Construction year: 1940
Manufacturer: London Midland Scottish Railway Company
Length: 19, 68 ft
Wide: 9, 51 ft
Height: 6, 98 ft
Weight: 17, 91 t
Speed: 29, 82 mph
Range: 93, 20 mi
Armour: 1, 57 in
Crew: 4

Tank Cruiser Mark III

Armament: 1 X 40 mm cannon, 1 X 7, 92 mm mg
Construction year: 1938
Manufacturer: Nuffield Mechanization & Aero Ltd.
Length: 19, 75 ft
Wide: 8, 33 ft
Height: 8, 49 ft
Weight: 13, 97 t
Speed: 29, 82 mph
Range: 93, 20 mi
Armour: 0, 55 in
Crew: 4

Tank Mark VII Tetrarch

Armament: 1 X 40 mm cannon, 1 X 7, 92 mm mg
Construction year: 1939
Manufacturer: Metro camel Works
Length: 14, 10 ft
Wide: 7, 57 ft
Height: 6, 95 ft
Weight: 7, 47 t
Speed: 39, 76 mph
Range: 111, 84 mi
Armour: 0, 39 in
Crew: 3

Tank TOG II

Armament: 1 X 77 mm cannon, 2 X 7, 92 mm mg
Construction year: 1940
Manufacturer: Foster & Metropolitan Carriage and Wagon Company
Length: 33, 23 ft
Wide: 10, 23 ft
Height: 9, 97 ft
Weight: 63, 48 t
Speed: 8, 07 mph
Range: 55, 92 mi
Armour: 2, 95 in
Crew: 5 – 6

Tank Mark III Valentine III

Armament: 1 X 40 mm cannon, 1 X 7, 92 mm mg
Construction year: 1941
Manufacturer: Vickers – Armstrong
Length: 17, 81 ft
Wide: 8, 62 ft
Height: 7, 44 ft
Weight: 15, 74 t
Speed: 14, 91 mph
Range: 90, 09 mi
Armour: 2, 36 in
Crew: 4

Tank Mark III Valentine VIII

Armament: 1 X 57 mm cannon, 2 X 7, 92 mm mg
Construction year: 1942
Manufacturer: Vickers – Armstrong
Length: 19, 38 ft
Wide: 8, 59 ft
Height: 7, 05 ft
Weight: 17, 12 t
Speed: 14, 91 mph
Range: 74, 56 mi
Armour: 2, 36 in
Crew: 3

Tank Cruiser Mark VI Crusader II

Armament: 1 X 40 mm cannon, 2 X 7, 92 mm mg
Construction year: 1940
Manufacturer: Nuffield Mechanisation & Awero Ltd.
Length: 19, 61 ft
Wide: 9, 05 ft
Height: 7, 31 ft
Weight: 18, 99 t
Speed: 27, 02 mph
Range: 198, 83 mi
Armour: 1, 96 in
Crew: 5

Tank Mark IV Churchill I

Armament: 1 X 40 mm cannon, 2 X 7, 29 mm mg, 1 X 76 mm cannon
Construction year: 1941
Manufacturer: Vauxhall Motor Company
Length: 24, 40 ft
Wide: 10, 66 ft
Height: 8, 10 ft
Weight: 37, 2 t
Speed: 16, 77 mph
Range: 126, 13 mi
Armour: 3, 97 in
Crew: 5

Tank Cruiser Mark VIII Cromwell VI

Armament: 1 X 75 mm cannon, 2 X 7, 92 mm mg
Construction year: 1942
Manufacturer: Birmingham Railway Carriage Company
Length: 21, 06 ft
Wide: 9, 54 ft
Height: 8, 23 ft
Weight: 27, 45 t
Speed: 39, 76 mph
Range: 172, 74 mi
Armour: 2, 99 in
Crew: 5

Tank Mark III Valentine XI

Armament: 1 X 75 mm cannon, 1 X 7, 92 mm mg
Construction year: 1943
Manufacturer: Vickers – Armstrong
Length: 17, 81 ft
Wide: 8, 62 ft
Height: 7, 57 ft
Weight: 18, 2 t
Speed: 14, 91 mph
Range: 77, 67 mi
Armour: 2, 95 in
Crew: 3

Tank Mark IV Churchill V

Armament: 1 X 95 mm cannon, 2 X 7, 92 mm mg
Construction year: 1942
Manufacturer: Vauxhall Motor Company
Length: 24, 44 ft
Wide: 10, 66 ft
Height: 6, 62 ft
Weight: 38, 97 t
Speed: 15, 53 mph
Range: 90, 09 mi
Armour: 4, 01 in
Crew: 5

Tank Mark IV Churchill VII

Armament: 1 X 75 mm cannon, 2 X 7, 92 mm mg
Construction year: 1944
Manufacturer: Vauxhall Motor Company
Length: 24, 44 ft
Wide: 11, 31 ft
Height: 9, 12 ft
Weight: 39, 95 t
Speed: 12, 42 mph
Range: 86, 99 mi
Armour: 5, 98 in
Crew: 5

Tank Challenger

Armament: 1 X 76, 2 mm cannon, 1 X 7, 92 mm mg
Construction year: 1943
Manufacturer: Birmingham Railway Carriage Company
Length: 26, 73 ft
Wide: 9, 51 ft
Height: 9, 15 ft
Weight: 32, 47 t
Speed: 27, 96 mph
Range: 119, 92 mi
Armour: 3, 97 in
Crew: 5

Tank Cruiser Comet

Armament: 1 X 77 mm cannon, 2 X 7, 92 mm mg
Construction year: 1944
Manufacturer: Leyland Motors Company
Length: 25, 09 ft
Wide: 10, 07 ft
Height: 8, 75 ft
Weight: 32, 67 t
Speed: 32 mph
Range: 149, 12 mi
Armour: 4, 01 in
Crew: 5

Tank Cruiser Centurion Mark I

Armament: 1 X 76, 2 mm cannon, 1 X 20 mm mg, 1 X 7, 92 mm mg
Construction year: 1945
Manufacturer: AEC
Length: 25, 16 ft
Height: 8, 98 ft
Weight: 47, 93 t
Speed: 21, 12 mph
Range: 59, 65 mi
Armour: 5, 98 in
Crew: 4

Tank Archer SP 17

Armament: 1 X 76, 2 mm cannon, 1 X 7, 7 mm mg
Construction year: 1943
Manufacturer: Vickers
Length: 21, 11 ft
Wide: 9, 05 ft
Height: 7, 38 ft
Weight: 14, 76 t
Speed: 20 mph
Range: 140 mi
Armour: 2, 36 in
Crew: 4

Tank Bishop

Armament: 1 X 87, 6 mm cannon
Construction year: 1941
Manufacturer: Birmingham Railway Carriage and Wagon Company
Length: 18, 50 ft
Wide: 9, 08 ft
Height: 10 ft
Weight: 7, 77 t
Speed: 15 mph
Range: 90 mi
Armour: 2, 36 in
Crew: 4

Tank Sexton

Armament: 1 X 87, 6 mm cannon
Construction year: 1941
Manufacturer: Montreal Locomotive Works
Length: 20, 07 ft
Wide: 8, 11 ft
Height: 8 ft
Weight: 25, 44 t
Speed: 25 mph
Range: 125 mi
Armour: 1, 25 in
Crew: 6

Tank CV 35/L3/35

Armament: 2 X 6, 5 mm or 8 mm mg
Construction year: 1935
Manufacturer: Ansaldo – Fossati
Length: 10, 33 ft
Wide: 4, 59 ft
Height: 4, 19 ft
Weight: 3, 05 t
Speed: 26, 09 mph
Range: 86, 99 mi
Armour: 0, 53 in
Crew: 2

Tank M 11/39

Armament: 1 X 37 mm cannon, 2 X 8 mm mg
Construction year: 1937
Manufacturer: Ansaldo – Fossati
Length: 15, 91 ft
Wide: 7, 15 ft
Height: 7, 38 ft
Weight: 10, 82 t
Speed: 19, 88 mph
Range: 130, 48 mi
Armour: 1, 18 in
Crew: 3

Tank M 13/40

Armament: 1 X 47 mm cannon, 3 X 8mm mg
Construction year: 1940
Manufacturer: Ansaldo – Fossati
Length: 16, 10 ft
Wide: 7, 21 ft
Height: 7, 77 ft
Weight: 13, 77 t
Speed: 18, 64 mph
Range: 124, 27 mi
Armour: 1, 57 in
Crew: 4

Tank M15/42

Armament: 1 X 47 mm cannon, 3 X 8 mm mg
Construction year: 1942
Manufacturer: Ansaldo – Fossati / Fiat
Length: 16, 60 ft
Wide: 7, 48 ft
Height: 7, 77 ft
Weight: 14, 76 t
Speed: 24, 85 mph
Range: 136, 7 mi
Armour: 1, 77 in
Crew: 4

Tank P 26/40

Armament: 1 X 75 mm cannon, 1 X 8 mm mg
Construction year: 1943
Manufacturer: Ansaldo – Fossati
Length: 18, 86 ft
Wide: 9, 02 ft
Height: 8, 20 ft
Weight: 24, 60 t
Speed: 24, 85 mph
Range: 173, 98 mi
Armour: 1, 96 in
Crew: 4

Tank L 6/40

Armament: 1 X 20 mm mg, 1 X 8 mm mg
Construction year: 1940
Manufacturer: Ansaldo – Fossati
Length: 12, 53 ft
Wide: 6, 10 ft
Height: 7, 11 ft
Weight: 6, 69 t
Speed: 26, 09 mph
Range: 124, 27 mi
Armour: 1, 57 in
Crew: 2

Tank Semovente da 75/18

Armament: 1 X 75 mm cannon, 1 X 8mm mg
Construction year: 1941
Manufacturer: Fiat – Ansaldo
Length: 16, 14 ft
Wide: 7, 21 ft
Height: 6, 06 ft
Weight: 14, 17 t
Speed: 19, 88 mph
Range: 142, 91 mi
Armour: 1, 96 in
Crew: 3

Tank Semovente 90/53

Armament: 1 X 90 mm cannon
Construction year: 1942
Manufacturer: Ansaldo
Length: 17, 32 ft
Wide: 7, 44 ft
Height: 7, 41 ft
Weight: 29, 52 t
Speed: 21, 74 mph
Range: 124, 27 mi
Armour: 1, 18 in
Crew: 4

Tank 95 Ha – Go

Armament: 1 X 37 mm cannon, 1 X 7, 7 mm mg
Construction year: 1935
Manufacturer: Mitsubishi
Length: 14, 1 ft
Wide: 6, 82 ft
Height: 7, 48 ft
Weight: 7, 28 t
Speed: 24, 85 mph
Range: 155, 34 mi
Armour: 0, 47 in
Crew: 3

Tank 97 Chi – Ha

Armament: 1 X 57 mm cannon, 2 X 7, 7 mm mg
Construction year: 1937
Manufacturer: Mitsubishi
Length: 18, 24 ft
Wide: 7, 64 ft
Height: 7, 31 ft
Weight: 14, 76 t
Speed: 23, 61 mph
Range: 130, 48 mi
Armour: 0, 66 in
Crew: 4

Tank 89 Chi – 10

Armament: 1 X 57 mm cannon, 2 X 7, 7 mm mg
Construction year: 1929
Manufacturer: Mitsubishi
Length: 18, 79 ft
Wide: 7, 15 ft
Height: 8, 46 ft
Weight: 11, 31 t
Speed: 14, 91 mph
Range: 86, 99 mi
Armour: 0, 66 in
Crew: 4

Tank 97 Te – Ke

Armament: 1 X 37 mm cannon
Construction year: 1939
Manufacturer: Tokyo
Length: 12, 17 ft
Wide: 6, 23 ft
Height: 5, 80 ft
Weight: 4, 62 t
Speed: 24, 85 mph
Range: 149, 12 mi
Armour: 0, 47 in
Crew: 4

Tank 94 Tankette

Armament: 1 X 6, 5 mm mg later 1 X 7, 7 mm mg
Construction year: 1932
Manufacturer: Hino Jidosha
Length: 9, 84 ft
Wide: 5, 24 ft
Height: 5, 24 ft
Weight: 3, 34 t
Speed: 25 mph
Range: 162 mi
Armour: 0, 47 in
Crew: 2

Tank 1 Chi – He

Armament: 1 X 47 mm cannon, 2 X 7, 7 mm mg
Construction year: 1940
Manufacturer: Mitsubishi
Length: 18, 04 ft
Wide: 7, 21 ft
Height: 7, 80 ft
Weight: 16, 73 t
Speed: 27 mph
Range: 130, 48 mi
Armour: 1, 96 in
Crew: 5

Tank Ho – Ni 1

Armament: 1 X 75 mm cannon
Construction year: 1942
Manufacturer: Mitsubishi
Length: 19, 35 ft
Wide: 7, 51 ft
Height: 7, 84 ft
Weight: 15, 15 t
Speed: 23, 61 mph
Range: 124, 27 mi
Armour: 2, 00 in
Crew: 5

Tank 92

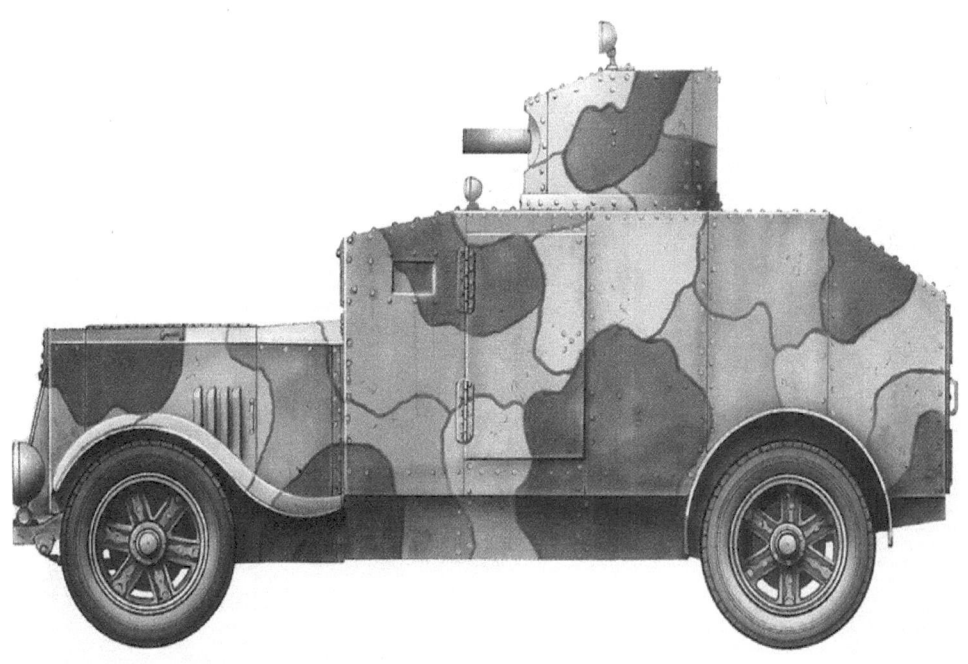

Armament: 1 X 36, 5 mm cannon
Construction year: 1932
Manufacturer: Ishikawajima Motorcar Factory
Length: 16, 40 ft
Wide: 6,06ft
Height: 9, 35 ft
Weight: 4, 42 t
Speed: 37,28mph
Range: 149,12 mi
Armour: 0, 39 in
Crew: 5

Tank 1 Ho – Ki

Armament: no
Construction year: 1941
Manufacturer: Hino Motors
Length: 15, 68 ft
Wide: 7, 18 ft
Height: 2, 58 ft
weight: 5, 41 t
Speed: 26, 09 mph
Range: 186, 41 mi
Armour: 0, 23 in
Crew: 2 + 12

Tank 1 Ho – Ha

Armament: 3 X 7, 7 mm mg
Construction year: 1941
Manufacturer: Hino Motors
Length: 20, 01 ft
Wide: 6, 88 ft
Height: 8, 23 ft
Weight: 6, 39 t
Speed: 31, 06 mph
Range: 186, 41 mi
Armour: 0, 31 in
Crew: 3 + 12

Tank 2 Ka – Mi

Speed: 22, 99 mph (street), 5, 90 mph (water)
Armament: 1 X 37 mm cannon, 2 X 7, 7 mm mg
Construction year: 1942
Manufacturer: Army's Sagami Arsenal
Length: 24, 34 ft
Wide: 9, 15 ft
Height: 7, 67 ft
Weight: 12, 10 t
Range: 124, 27 mi
Armour: 0, 51 in
Crew: 6

Tank 3 Ka – Chi

Speed: 19, 88 mph (street),   6, 21 mph (water)
Armament: 1 X 47 mm cannon, 2 X 7, 7 mm mg
Construction year: 1942
Manufacturer: Hino Motors
Length: 33, 79 ft
Wide: 9, 84 ft
Height: 12, 53 ft
Weight: 28, 24 t
Range: 198, 83 mi
Armour: 1, 96 in
Crew: 7

Amphibious vehicle 4 Ka – Tsu

Speed: 12, 42 mph (street), 4, 97 mph (water)
Armament: 2 torpedoes, 2, 13 mm mg
Construction year: 1942
Manufacturer: Hino Motors
Length: 36, 08 ft
Wide: 10, 82 ft
Height: 9, 81 ft
Weight: 15, 74 t
Range: unknown mi
Armour: 0, 39 in
Crew: 6 + 40

Tank 98 So – Da

Armament: no
Construction year: 1938
Manufacturer: Tokyo
Length: 12, 46 ft
Wide: 6, 23 ft
Height: 5, 25 ft
Weight: 4, 92 t
Speed: 24, 85 mph
Range: 124, 27 mi
Armour: 0, 47 in
Crew: 2 + 10

Tank 100 Te – Re

Armament: no
Construction year: 1940
Manufacturer: Mitsubishi
Length: 13, 35 ft
Wide: 6, 52 ft
Height: 6, 23 ft
Weight: 4, 82 t
Speed: 24, 85 mph
Range: 124, 27 mi
Armour: 0, 23 in
Crew: 8

Specal thanks to:

U.S. Department of the Army

U.S. Naval Academy

U.S. Department of Defense

U.S. Department of the Navy

1 st Armored Division

9 st Armored Division

12 th Armoured Brigade

Royal Scot Dragoon Guards

The Kings Royal Hussars